W9-AHR-582

A PICTURE BOOK OF
Sam Houston

by David A. Adler *and* Michael S. Adler
illustrated by Matt Collins

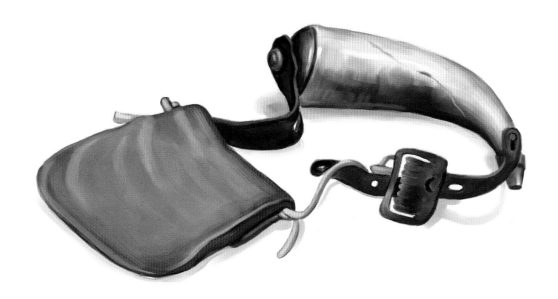

Holiday House / New York

The people of Texas were fighting for their country's independence from Mexico. In March 1836 almost two hundred Texan soldiers took a stand in an abandoned Spanish mission, the Alamo, in San Antonio. They were surrounded by almost two thousand Mexican soldiers.

"Fight to the very last," Texas Colonel William B. Travis told his men.

They did.

Every Texan soldier at the Alamo was killed— one hundred and eighty-nine—including Travis, Davy Crockett, and Jim Bowie. Texans never forgot this battle.

The commander in chief of the small Texas army was a tall, powerful man named Sam Houston. Prospects were bleak. Then, on April 21, 1836, he and his men were by the San Jacinto River surrounded by Mexican soldiers.

"We are Texans," Houston told his men. "If you wish to fight, here is your chance and now is the time. . . . Remember the Alamo!"

With that battle cry Houston led his men into battle.

Within just eighteen minutes the fight was over. Houston and his men had done what seemed impossible. They had defeated a huge force of well-armed soldiers. Texas was on its way to independence.

Sam Houston was born on March 2, 1793, in Rockbridge County, Virginia. He was the fifth of nine children born to Samuel and Elizabeth Houston.

His father was a farmer and a soldier in the Revolutionary War. His mother was the daughter of one of Rockbridge County's richest men.

In early spring 1807 the Houston family moved west, to a farm near Maryville, Tennessee.

At sixteen Sam left home and moved to an island in the middle of the Tennessee River. The island was occupied by Cherokee Indians. He lived there for three years and learned to speak, dress, and hunt like a Cherokee. He embraced American Indian legends. They called him Co-lon-neh, the Raven. Houston later said his time there "fitted me for my destiny," that it was his "molding period of life."

Houston was confident of his abilities. In 1812, even though he had very little formal schooling, he opened his own school in Maryville. He made himself headmaster and soon had a room full of tuition-paying students.

At the age of twenty he became a soldier. He joined the Tennessee Regulars to fight against the British in the War of 1812. He was a brave fighter. An arrow hit him in his leg and he kept fighting. In another battle three bullets hit him. Sadly, his war wounds never fully healed.

General Andrew Jackson greatly admired Houston's bravery. He helped get him a job with the U.S. War Department.

In 1818 Houston moved to Nashville. He studied law and set up a law office. He was soon appointed attorney general of Nashville and given command of the state militia. Four years later he was elected to the United States House of Representatives. In 1827 he was elected governor of Tennessee.

In January 1829 Governor Houston married Eliza Allen, but the marriage lasted just three months. The people of Tennessee felt the breakup of his marriage shamed the state. On April 16, 1829, he resigned as governor.

He returned to the Cherokees, where he met and married Tiana Rogers Gentry, a recent widow; but they soon divorced.

Houston was married for a third time, on May 9, 1840, to Margaret Lea. This marriage lasted. "Every hour we are apart," he wrote the first time he was away, "resolves me, more firmly, not again to be separated from you." They had eight children together.

In the early 1830s, Texas was ruled by Mexico. Many of the Americans who lived there felt mistreated. They were set on independence. The Mexican leader, Antonio López de Santa Anna, was determined to crush their resistance. President Jackson sent Houston to Texas to convince the American Indians to fight alongside the Americans.

The Convention of 1836 issued the Texas Declaration of Independence. Houston's signature on it was big and bold. The leaders of the new republic chose him to lead the army. He left the convention wearing a Cherokee coat, a buckskin vest, and a broad-brimmed hat with a large feather in its band.

He gathered men for his army. After the stunning victory at San Jacinto, the defeated Santa Anna signed a treaty granting Texas independence.

Sam Houston was elected the first president of the Republic of Texas. He was president from 1836 to 1838 and again from 1841 to 1844. He kept peace with the American Indians and won recognition for the new republic from his friend President Andrew Jackson. He also saw the nation's capital moved to a city founded in 1836 and named Houston in his honor.

Houston knew the young nation would have trouble defending itself from Mexican threats and wanted Texas to become part of the United States. In 1845 Congress passed a resolution making Texas the twenty-eighth state.

The next year Sam Houston was elected to the United States Senate, a position he held for thirteen years.

During Houston's years in the Senate the issue of slavery divided the nation. Houston was against slavery. His position was not popular in Texas.

There were compromises that temporarily resolved the slavery dispute, but Houston didn't think the peace would last. "A nation divided against itself cannot stand," he said in an 1850 speech, quoting the Bible. Eight years later President Abraham Lincoln quoted the same verse.

In 1859 Houston left the Senate and was elected governor of Texas. In 1861 the Texas legislature voted to secede from the Union and become part of a new nation, the Confederate States of America.

"Let me tell you what is coming," Houston said. "After the sacrifice of countless millions of treasure and hundreds of thousands of lives," the North "will overwhelm the South."

Houston was asked to take a loyalty oath to the Confederacy.

"I love Texas too much to bring strife and bloodshed upon her," he wrote. "I refuse to take this oath."

He was forced out of office.

Houston retired. He and his wife, Margaret, moved to Huntsville, Texas. He was still a favorite of many Texans. He gave speeches but said "under no circumstances" would he ever run again for office.

Sam Houston had commanded an army. He had been a governor, a
senator, and the president of Texas.

On July 26, 1863, Sam Houston died from pneumonia. In his last breaths
he called out his two great loves, "Texas! Texas! Margaret!"

"He has risen to the throne of power," a Houston newspaper wrote at his
death. "Let us shed tears to his memory, tears that are due to one who has
filled so much of our affections."

IMPORTANT DATES

1793   Born in Rockbridge County, Virginia, March 2.

1807   The Houston family moves to Maryville, Tennessee.

1809   Begins to live with the Cherokee Nation. He is given the name Raven and learns to speak, dress, and hunt like a Cherokee.

1812   Returns to Maryville and founds a one-room schoolhouse.

1813   Fights in the War of 1812 and in 1814 is severely injured.

1818   Moves to Nashville, studies law, and sets up a law office.

1822   Elected to the United States House of Representatives.

1827   Elected governor of Tennessee.

1829   Marries Eliza Allen.

1830   Marries Tiana Rogers Gentry.

1836   Made commander in chief of the Texas army. Elected the first president of the Republic of Texas.

1840   Marries Margaret Lea. They have eight children.

1845   Texas enters the Union as its twenty-eighth state, December 29.

1861   Texas legislature votes to secede from the Union and join the Confederacy.

1863   Dies in Huntsville, Texas, July 26.

SOURCE NOTES

Each source note includes the first word or words and the last word or words of a quotation and its source. References are to books cited in the Selected Bibliography.

"Fight to the very last": Evans, p. 319.

"We are Texans . . . the Alamo!": Evans, p. 322.

"fitted me . . . molding period of life.": Williams, p. 26.

"Every hour we . . . separated from you.": James, p. 314.

"A nation . . . cannot stand": Braider, p. 260.
When Lincoln quoted the verse, he translated it as
"A house divided against itself cannot stand."

"Let me tell . . . overwhelm the South.": James, pp. 409–410.

"I love Texas . . . to take this oath.": James, p. 412.

"under no circumstances": Williams, p. 359.

"Texas! . . . Margaret!": James, p. 433.

"He has risen . . . of our affections.": Williams, p. 363.

SELECTED BIBLIOGRAPHY

Braider, Donald. *Solitary Star: A Biography of Sam Houston*. New York: Putnam, 1974.

Evans, Lawton B. *America First*. Springfield, MA: Milton Bradley, 1920.

Flanagan, Sue. *Sam Houston's Texas*. Austin: University of Texas Press, 1964.

Friend, Llerena. *Sam Houston: The Great Designer*. Austin: University of Texas Press, 1989.

Fritz, Jean. *Make Way for Sam Houston*. New York: Putnam, 1986.

James, Marquis. *The Raven: A Biography of Sam Houston*. Garden City, N.Y.: Halcyon House, 1929.

Williams, John Hoyt. *Sam Houston*. New York: Simon and Schuster, 1993.

RECOMMENDED WEBSITES

www.lone-star.net / mall / texasinfo / shouston.htm

www.tshaonline.org / handbook / online / articles / fho73

http: / hotx.com / alamo / houston.html

www.spartacus.schoolnet.co.uk / WWhoustonS.htm

For Mom and Dad Oppenheim with thanks—M. S. A.

For Captain Zach Watson—M. C.

Text copyright © 2012 by David A. Adler and Michael S. Adler
Illustrations copyright © 2012 by Matt Collins
All Rights Reserved
HOLIDAY HOUSE is registered in the U.S. Patent and Trademark Office.
Printed and Bound in November 2011 at Tien Wah Press, Johor Bahru, Johor, Malaysia.
The text typeface is Palatino.
The artwork was created in Corel Painter.
www.holidayhouse.com
First Edition
1 3 5 7 9 10 8 6 4 2

Library of Congress Cataloging-in-Publication Data
Adler, David A.
A picture book of Sam Houston / by David A. Adler and Michael S. Adler ; illustrated by Matt Collins. — 1st ed.
p. cm.
ISBN 978-0-8234-2369-9 (hardcover)
1. Houston, Sam, 1793-1863—Juvenile literature.
2. Governors—Texas—Biography—Juvenile literature.
3. Legislators—United States—Biography—Juvenile literature.
4. United States. Congress. Senate—Biography—Juvenile literature.
5. Texas—History—To 1846—Juvenile literature.
I. Adler, Michael S. II. Collins, Matt, ill. III. Title.
F390.H84A45 2012
976.4'04092—dc23
[B]
2011007265